Paul.

£2.50

KU-350-209

THE ST JOHN RIVER VALLEY

THE ST JOHN RIVER VALLEY

Photographs by Wayne Barrett and Anne MacKay
Introduction by George MacBeath

Toronto
OXFORD UNIVERSITY PRESS
1981

Title page and back jacket FIDDLEHEADS AM

Designed by FORTUNATO AGLIALORO

©Oxford University Press (Canadian Branch) 1981
ISBN 0-19-540339-8
1 2 3 4 - 3 2 1 0
Printed in Hong Kong by
EVERBEST PRINTING COMPANY LIMITED

INTRODUCTION
by George MacBeath

I come from the green pine forests,
Where nature runs wild and free,—
From the haunt of the moose, and deer, and wolf,
To the gray and restless Sea.

H. L. Spencer

THE ST JOHN IS A MAGNIFICENT RIVER. Even to those who know it well, it is ever changing, ever new—now revealing vistas of extreme beauty, now tumbling furiously over falls and rapids, now languishing and placid. Never is it without interest.

The mighty St John is one of the most famous rivers in Canada. It draws its strength from an immense and well-watered area as it flows 450 miles through Maine and New Brunswick, finally emptying into the Bay of Fundy. From prehistoric times it served the Indians and white couriers in turn as the main inland route between Quebec and the Maritimes.

It is the countless brooks and streams that vein the woodlands of northern Maine that come together to give the river its lusty origins. From its source at the headwaters of Baker Brook along the 181 miles to Edmundston, the St John flows swiftly and eagerly and during most of the year is navigable only by canoe. Edmundston—the Petit Sault (Little Falls) of former days—is New Brunswick's most northern city and is largely French-speaking. It is a lumbering centre, the lively hub of the northwestern portion of the Province. Between Edmundston and Grand Falls, a distance of 36 miles, the St John becomes slow-moving and can be navigated by vessels of shoal draft for most of the summer season. Along this stretch tiny up-river settlements dot the shores, interspersed with thick forest

growth and peaceful farms set amid gently rolling fields.

At Grand Falls the river drops 75 feet over a ledge of slate and limestone in one of Canada's great cascades, then continues on its way in a petulant mood. Over the next 130 miles the often treacherous water is broken by projecting sand bars, swift-running rips and rapids, and the hydro-electric dam at Beechwood. Here one experiences the essence of the St John and its valley—a marvellous agricultural, recreational, and scenic resource. And ever present are the friendly villages and towns: the Indian village of Maliseet; Perth-Andover at the mouth of the tributary Tobique; Hartland and the world's longest covered bridge; and charming Woodstock—centre of the potato country—with its beautifully restored county courthouse. About forty miles farther down, following the broad twists and turns of the now-placid river, is Kings Landing historical settlement. This meticulous recreation of a typical riverside community of the central St John valley of a century and more ago, now celebrated as an outdoor museum, transports visitors back to an earlier day on the venerable river.

Ten miles below Kings Landing is Mactaquac Dam, the most important hydro-electric installation in New Brunswick. Its construction in the 1960s created a headpond, or lake, more than 55 miles in length. Around its edge are to be found some of the Province's best recreational facilities, highlighted by the 1,400-acre Mactaquac Provincial Park.

At Springhill, four miles above Fredericton, the gentle ebb and flow of tide can first be felt. As if soothed by this rhythmic promise of the sea, the St John, now some 90 miles from its mouth in the Atlantic, slackens its pace. It broadens until it is three quarters of a mile wide at Fredericton, New Brunswick's beautiful capital. The St John flows through the very centre of the 'Cathedral City'; on its banks stand the Beaverbrook Gallery and the Playhouse, the Officers Quarters and Men's Barracks from British Army days, and historic Old Government House. A little farther back is the University of New Brunswick's Art Building, the oldest university building in Canada.

Then comes the final stretch of the river. Fed in quick succession by many smaller rivers, chief among them being the Salmon River, and by Grand Lake, Washademoak Lake, Belleisle Bay, and the Nerepis and Kennebecasis Rivers, the St John deepens quickly. It has been said that no one can have seen New Brunswick who has not travelled the magnificent river route between Fredericton and Saint John. Among the vivid memories of my boyhood are the trips I occasionally took by steamboat on the lower river. Though the steamboats are gone, it is still easy to recapture those hours, for much of this majestic river's awesome beauty is still unspoiled. It is this section, with its thirty-two islands, broken shoreline, and beautiful hills, that has provided the setting for a great deal of our most exciting history. Oromocto, site of Canadas largest military base, historic Maugerville and Sheffield, Gagetown and that shiretown's impressive grouping of early buildings, Evandale and Hampstead, are all part of that history. (Here one is particularly struck by the realization that the valley is the richest agricultural area of the Province.) Nothing disturbs the river's deep and steady flow towards the Bay, and it is passable for vessels of large tonnage.

At its mouth nature presents the St John with a challenge: it must force its way through a narrow 200-yard gorge, crossed by a shoal ledge and choked with huge rocks and small islands. And the tide, whose regular ebb and flow give it a pulse, suddenly becomes its enemy. The battle enacted by these two great, natural forces, the Bay of Fundy tide and the mighty St John River, wages around the clock. For six hours the tide, often reaching 30 feet, holds and presses back the river; then it wanes and for the next six hours the river presses forward with water foaming and deep whirlpools, until at low tide it falls seventeen feet into the Bay. Only during that short period of slack tide, when the two forces are equal, can any vessel navigate the Reversing Falls.

Saint John, the port city that developed at the mouth of the river, has the distinction of being the first city in British North America to be incorporated by Royal Charter, an event that took place in 1785. From its beginning Saint John had a flourishing seaboard trade. As the fishing and shipbuilding trades grew, so did the population; artisans and craftsmen were attracted there as citizens, and commercial control of the river was secured. Today Saint John is New Brunswick's largest city and the home of such landmarks as the New Brunswick Museum, the Martello Tower, the Loyalist House, and the Old City Market, with its captivating stalls that feature country produce, meats, fish, and crafts from the area.

It is fitting that Saint John should bear the name that was given to the river back in 1604. It was on St John the Baptist Day, 24 June, in that year that the French explorers Samuel de Champlain and Pierre de Monts, who had been granted a monopoly of the fur trade, first saw it. Long before that it had been known as 'Woolastook', meaning 'good river', the name given to it by the Maliseet Indians, whose forebears were the first human inhabitants of the St John valley, having come there as nomadic hunters more than 11,000 years before. Over the many centuries before the white man arrived, the Indians who roamed this lovely, wild valley, hunting and fishing, travelled the length of the waterway in their birch-bark canoes.

Following the discovery of the St John in 1604, Europeans developed an interest in the river. Its lure was the wealth of the fur trade, and colourful pages of history recount conflicts and heroics—including those of the French noblemen Charles de la Tour and d'Aulnay de Charnisay. In time large land grants, which together comprised the entire valley, were distributed, but few even temporary communities resulted. As the struggle for America unfolded, conflict between English and French caused settlement to languish until 1758.

It was in that year the French were driven from the lower St John by a force under General Robert Monckton, and the river valley, still a largely untouched wilderness, came under British control. Four years later hamlets were established by New Englanders in Maugerville and at the mouth of the river. The fertile land produced an abundant harvest, but greater attention was given in those years to a rich export of furs, timber, and fish. In 1779 masting and ship-timber operations began, much of the product being floated to the river's mouth for shipment to England.

In 1783 the arrival in the St John valley of some ten thousand Loyalists, refugees from the new United States, brought about the first effective settlement of the territory. It was then that the city of Saint John came into being at the mouth of the river, several tiny communities emerged in the valley, and the capital of a new province was established at Fredericton, site of the former French settlement of Sainte-Anne. For the Loyalists, and other settlers from England, Scotland, Ireland, and the United States who wrested a place for themselves in this land, the river served as the vital communications and transportation link to these new valley settlements. Fields were cleared, dwellings erected, agriculture and lumbering developed. The towboat, scow, woodboat, and lumber raft became familiar sights as trade grew and settlement spread. The river was indeed a busy scene, with its remarkable variety of watercraft, including steamboats, which dominated transportation on the St John for 131 years.

As time passed and settlement grew, communications along the St John became more dependable. From the metropolis of Saint John to the vigorous Acadian French communities that had developed along the upper river, expanding and improved roads made inland transportation easier. Gradually motor vehicles and locomotives reached all the valley communities, and eventually captured the bulk of the carrying trade. The St John thereby lost its dominance as the key communications and transportation link in the valley. Yet it has retained its importance, finding new roles as a recreational mecca, a vital source of electricity, and as a veritable life force to both man and nature within its valley.

How does one depict a river such as the magnificent St John? The challenge Wayne Barrett and Anne McKay set themselves was to portray the very essence of the river. During untold hours of travel over a period of nearly two years, they photographed its physical features, its variety, and its moods. The result is a loving and painstaking collection of views of the St John and its valley, from its headwaters to its union with the Bay of Fundy. Being true artists, they capture the river's timeless quality, the sense of its flowing through history. Their appreciation of its physical appearance and changing face, and of the life to be found along the banks of this celebrated waterway—so aptly described as the backbone of New Brunswick—is evident in all their photographs. For me, savouring this pictorial essay has been a delight, one that I hope you too may share.

1 Glacier Lake AM

2 Near Grand Falls AM
3 Grand Falls WB

4 St Francis, Maine WB
5 Hatfield Point AM

6   Upper St John, Maine WB
7   Gagetown AM

8   Near Hatfield Point AM
9   Saint-Francois-de-Madawaska WB

10   **Baker Brook** AM

11 Saint-Hilaire, looking across into Maine WB

12   Lac Baker AM

13 Near River de Chute AM

14 Lac Baker WB
15 Hatfield Point WB

16   Baker Brook WB

17 Edmundston WB

18   Bear Island WB
19   Keswick AM

20   Saint-Hilaire WB
21   Near Grand Falls WB

22   Mactaquac WB
23   Keswick AM

24 Spring flooding near Maugerville WB
25 Bayswater WB

26 Sheffield AM
27 Holderville AM

28 Sheffield from Oromocto WB
29 Queenstown WB

30 Wickham AM
31 Keswick Ridge WB

32 Hampstead WB
33 Nackawic AM

34 Kings Landing AM
35 World's longest covered bridge, Hartland WB

37   Wickham AM

38 Near McGowan's Corner WB
39 Near Wickham AM

40 Jemseg, near Grand Lake WB
41 Long Reach WB

42 Fredericton AM
43 Fredericton AM

44 Fredericton WB
45 Fredericton AM

46   Legislative Building, Fredericton WB

47   Fredericton WB

48 The Green, Fredericton AM
49 Military Compound, Fredericton WB

50 Fredericton WB
51 Christ Church Cathedral, Fredericton WB

52 & 53   Near Florenceville AM

54 Wickham AM
55 McGowan's Corner AM

56 Woodstock AM
57 Near Hatfield Point AM

58   Hampstead WB
59   Ferry, Belle Isle Bay WB

60   Gagetown WB
61   Evandale AM

62 McGowan's Corner WB
63 Jemseg AM

64 Jemseg AM
65 Saint-Basile AM

66 Maugerville AM

67   Hartland AM

70   Belleisle Bay AM

71 Along the Kennebecasis WB

72   King Square, Saint John WB
73   St John estuary from the Martello Tower AM

74 Saint John AM
75 Saint John WB

76 Irving Refinery, Saint John WB
77 Drydock, Saint John WB

78   Harbour, Saint John AM
79   Reversing Falls, Saint John AM
80   *(over)* Longs Creek AM